Mighty Machines

Ambulances

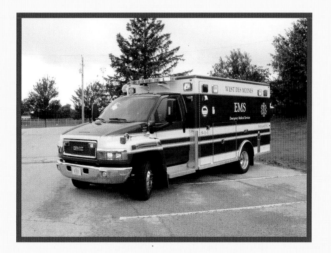

by Carol K. Lindeen

Consulting Editor: Gail Saunders-Smith, PhD

Capstone
press

Mankato, Minnesota

Pebble Plus is published by Capstone Press,
151 Good Counsel Drive, P.O. Box 669, Mankato, Minnesota 56002.
www.capstonepress.com

1 2 3 4 5 6 10 09 08 07 06 05

Library of Congress Cataloging-in-Publication Data
Lindeen, Carol K., 1976–
    Ambulances / by Carol K. Lindeen.
    p. cm.—(Pebble plus: mighty machines)
    Includes bibliographical references and index.
    ISBN 0-7368-3652-7 (hardcover)
    ISBN 0-7368-5137-2 (softcover)
1. Ambulances—Juvenile literature. I. Title. II. Series.
TL235.8.L56 2005
362.18'8—dc22   2004014916

Summary: Simple text and photographs present ambulances, their parts, and how emergency crews
use ambulances.

Editorial Credits
Mari C. Schuh, editor; Molly Nei, set designer; Kate Opseth and Ted Williams, book designers;
  Jo Miller, photo researcher; Scott Thoms, photo editor

Photo Credits
Capstone Press/Gary Sundermeyer, 19; Karon Dubke, cover
Corbis/Gabe Palmer, 6–7; Royalty-Free, 5
Daniel E. Hodges, 1, 9
Folio Inc./Novastock, 10–11
Getty Images Inc./The Image Bank/Pat LaCroix, 13
Index Stock Imagery/Mark Gibson, 20–21; Omni Photo Communications Inc., 14–15
911 Pictures, 17

**Pebble Plus thanks the Gold Cross Ambulance Service of Mankato, Minnesota, for its assistance
with photo shoots.**

Note to Parents and Teachers

The Mighty Machines set supports national standards related to science, technology, and society. This book describes and illustrates ambulances. The images support early readers in understanding the text. The repetition of words and phrases helps early readers learn new words. This book also introduces early readers to subject-specific vocabulary words, which are defined in the Glossary section. Early readers may need assistance to read some words and to use the Table of Contents, Glossary, Read More, Internet Sites, and Index sections of the book.

Table of Contents

What Are Ambulances?

Ambulances are vehicles
that take hurt or sick people
to hospitals.

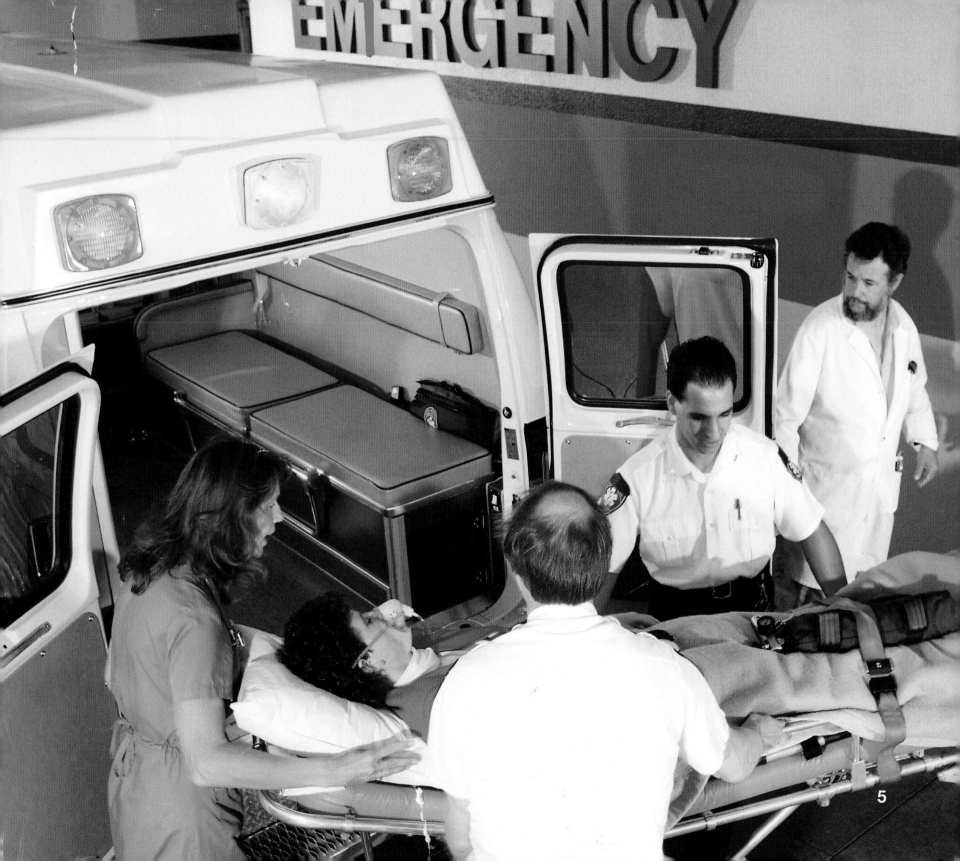

Ambulance Parts

Ambulances have
flashing lights and sirens.
They warn people that
an ambulance is coming.

Ambulance drivers

sit in cabs. They talk

on the ambulance radio.

They turn on

the sirens and lights.

Hurt or sick people

ride in the back

of ambulances.

Supplies sit on shelves.

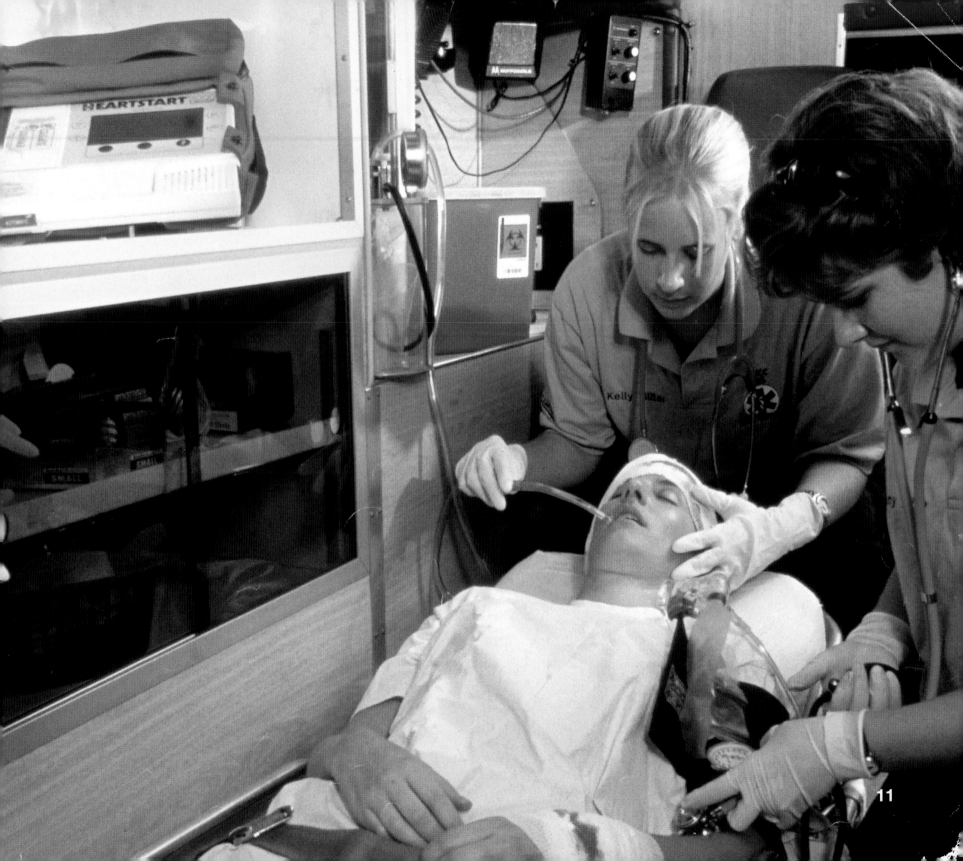

To the Rescue

An ambulance worker
gets a call on the radio.
Someone is hurt.

The driver turns on
the sirens and lights.
The ambulance rushes
down the street.

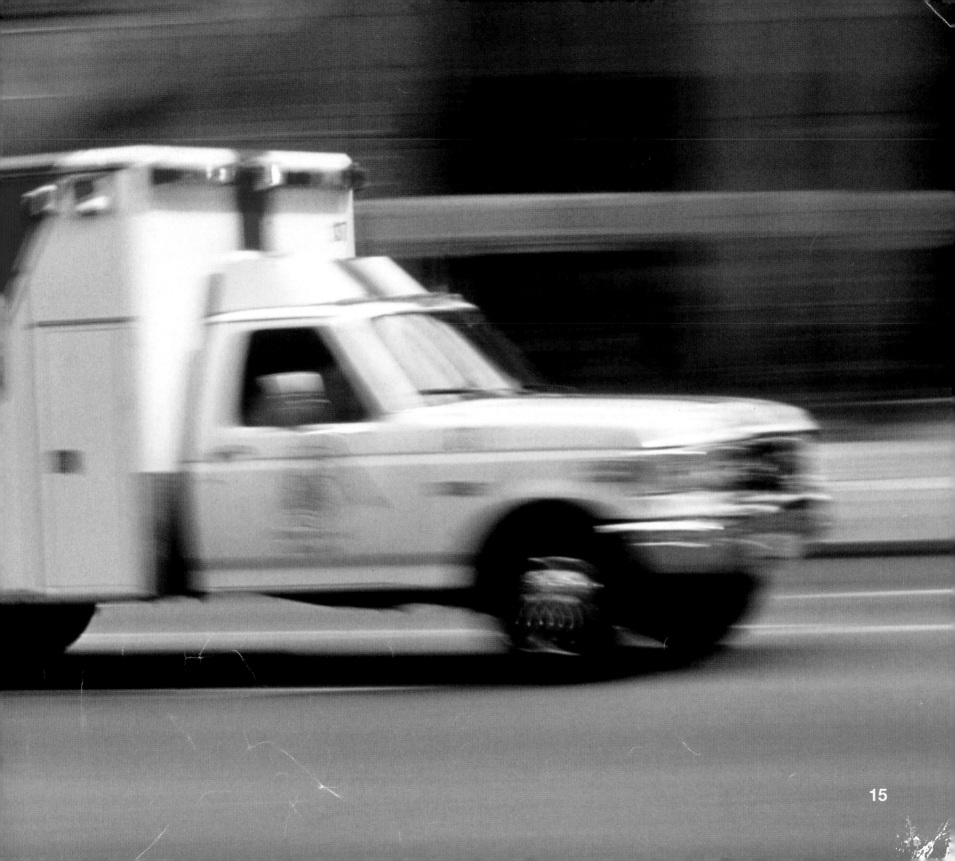

The workers put the patient

on a stretcher.

They lift the stretcher

into the ambulance.

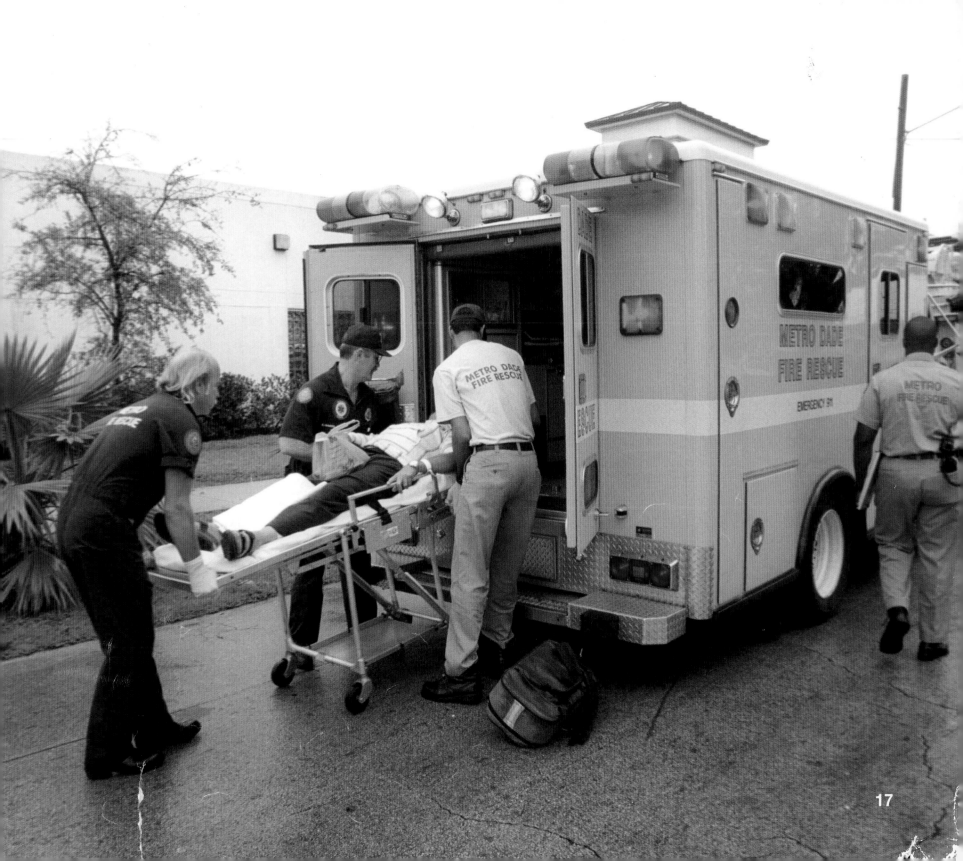

A worker takes care
of the patient.
The ambulance rushes
to the hospital.

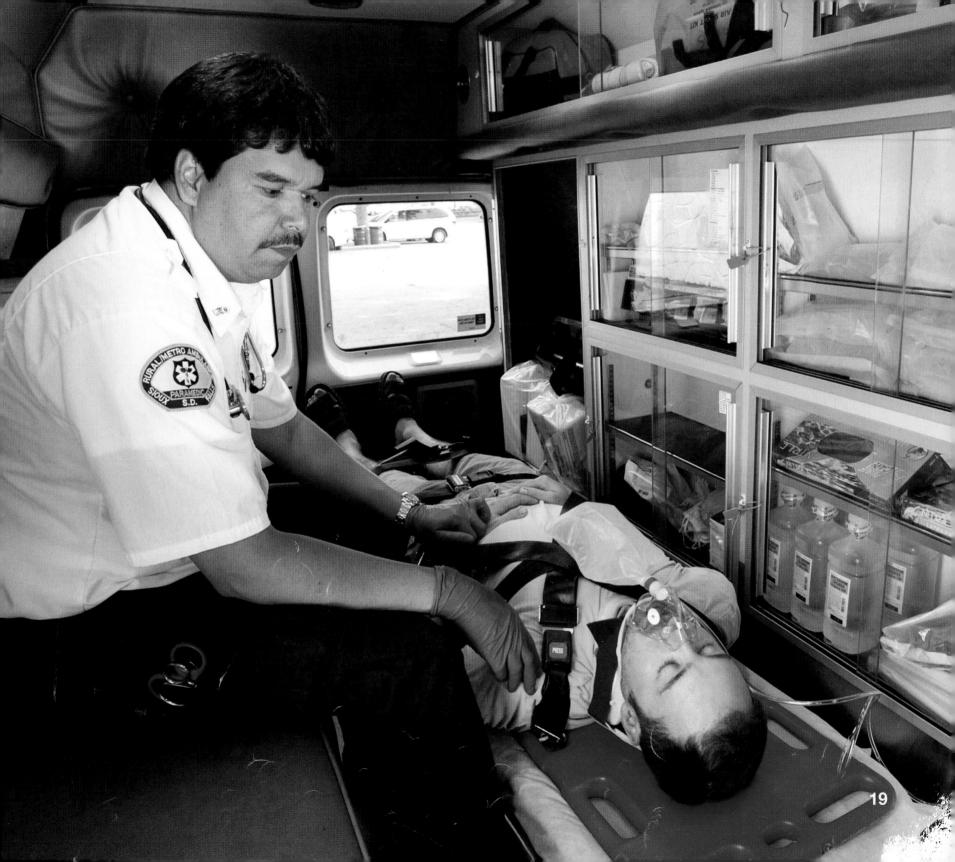

Workers use ambulances
to help people
in emergencies.

Glossary

cab—the driver's area of a large truck or machine

emergency—something that happens with no warning and requires action right away

hospital—a place where doctors and nurses take care of sick or hurt people

patient—a person who is waiting for or getting medical care

siren—an object that makes a very loud sound as a warning

stretcher—a bed with wheels and legs that fold up; patients are strapped onto stretchers while in the ambulance.

vehicle—something that carries people or goods from one place to another; ambulances, police cars, and fire trucks are types of vehicles.

Read More

Gordon, Sharon. *What's inside an Ambulance?* What's Inside. New York: Benchmark Books, 2004.

Hanson, Anne E. *Ambulances.* The Transportation Library. Mankato, Minn.: Bridgestone Books, 2001.

Levine, Michelle. *Ambulances.* Pull Ahead Books. Minneapolis: Lerner, 2004.

Internet Sites

FactHound offers a safe, fun way to find Internet sites related to this book. All of the sites on FactHound have been researched by our staff.

Here's how:

1. Visit *www.facthound.com*

2. Type in this special code **0736836527** for age-appropriate sites. Or enter a search word related to this book for a more general search.

3. Click on the **Fetch It** button.

FactHound will fetch the best sites for you!

Index

Word Count: 119
Grade: 1
Early-Intervention Level: 14

The Conflict Resolution Library™

Dealing with Bullying

• Marianne Johnston •

The Rosen Publishing Group's

PowerKids Press™

New York

Published in 1996 by The Rosen Publishing Group, Inc.
29 East 21st Street, New York, NY 10010

Copyright © 1996 by The Rosen Publishing Group, Inc.

First Edition

Book design: Kim Sonsky

Photo credits: Cover by Seth Dinnerman; p. 20 © Mimi Cotter/International Stock; all other photos by Seth Dinnerman.

Johnston, Marianne.
    Dealing with bullying / Marianne Johnston.
        p.   cm. — (The conflict resolution library)
    Includes index.
    Summary: Describes what is meant by bullying then goes on to explain why bullies act as they do, how to deal with them, and how to stop being one.
    ISBN 0-8239-2374-6
    1. Bullying—Juvenile literature. [1. Bullying.　2. Bullies.]
    I. Title. II. Series.
BF637-B85J64 1996
303.6'9—dc20

95-20209
CIP
AC

Manufactured in the United States of America

Contents

What Is a Bully?

Do you know someone who seems to enjoy hurting or scaring others? Maybe there is someone like that at your school. Maybe you have an older brother who acts that way. Maybe you've acted that way toward a younger sister.

Someone who **intimidates** (in-TIM-ih-dayts) and hurts others is a **bully** (BUL-lee). Even though a bully may seem happy when he hurts someone, he really isn't. It may seem strange, but bullies are usually unhappy.

◀ Bullies scare or hurt other people to try to make themselves feel good.

Words Hurt Too

Some bullies scare people with their fists. Others scare people with their words. Has anyone ever told you, "I'll hurt you if you don't do what I want"? When a bully does this, she is **threatening** (THREH-tin-ing) you. Many bullies use **threats** (THRETS) to scare people. Some bullies say mean things and **insult** (in-SULT) people just to make them feel bad. A bully who uses words can be just as mean and scary as one who uses fists. Sometimes a threat or an insult can hurt more than a punch.

The things that a bully says can hurt you just as much as if she had hit you. ▶

Why Do People Bully Others?

Bullies act the way they do for different reasons. Sometimes someone is being mean to them. Maybe the bully has an older brother or other family member who treats him badly. So he treats others the same way. That way he doesn't feel as if *he* is being bullied. Other bullies are scared, lonely, or afraid that other people won't like them. They think that if they show everyone how tough they are, no one will know how scared or lonely they are.

◀ Some bullies treat others the way they are treated by older sisters or brothers.

Self-Esteem

Most bullies have low **self-esteem** (SELF-es-TEEM). They don't like themselves very much. So bullies hurt and insult other people. That makes a bully feel better. Then he isn't the only one who is hurt and upset. Sometimes bullies are jealous of other people's **accomplishments** (uh-KOM-plish-mints). They get **frustrated** (FRUS-tray-tid) because they don't feel that they are good at anything. So they rely on scaring other people, the one skill they know they have.

Sometimes bullies feel jealous of others. ▶

How to Deal with a Bully

A bully wants you to get angry. He may even want you to fight with him. Try walking away from the bully. If he still bothers you, tell him firmly to leave you alone.

If this doesn't work, tell a grown-up. The grown-up may be able to help the bully understand why he acts the way he does. Then the bully will be able to change his behavior.

◀ One way to deal with a bully is to walk away from him.

How to Stop Being a Bully

Do you ever bully other people? Do you feel powerful when you hurt or scare someone who is smaller than you? If you do, think about why you do it. Maybe someone is bullying you. Maybe you're not happy with yourself. Maybe you are scared that other people won't like you. If you are a bully, try talking to a grown-up about why you are a bully. That grown-up may be able to help you find other ways to feel good about yourself. You'll find that it's a lot more fun to be friends with someone than to bully her.

Talk to an adult about why ▶
you bully other people.

Helping Someone Else

If you see a bully giving someone a hard time, try to help. Don't try to fight the bully. But stand behind the person being bullied. There is strength in numbers. A bully is most **comfortable** (KUMF-ter-bul) when he is **confronting** (kun-FRUN-ting) one person. Bullies only fight when there is no chance they'll get hurt. When there is more than one person, even if they are both smaller, the bully will most likely back off. You can also help by calling over an adult, such as a parent or a teacher.

◀ When a bully realizes that he is outnumbered, he will probably leave you both alone.

Jason the Bully

Jason had been the school bully for as long as Cory could remember. One day, Cory saw Jason pushing a younger kid around on the playground. Cory was smaller than Jason, but he decided to go over and help. He calmly told Jason to leave the kid alone. When Jason threatened him, Cory did not fight back. He told Jason that they were not going to fight. Jason saw that he was out-numbered. He decided to leave the playground.

You can help someone who is being bullied just by being there. ▶

Helping a Bully

The next step is to try to help the bully. If a person has been a bully for a long time, she probably doesn't have many friends. Chances are no one has said a nice word to her for a long time.

Being kind to a former bully will make her feel better about herself. Show her that you will be her friend if she will stop being so mean. Bullies are just like everyone else. They want to be liked and accepted too.

◀ Being kind to a bully may help her stop being so mean. You may even make a new friend.

Not a Bully Anymore

The next day, Cory saw Jason in the hallway at school. He asked Jason what his favorite sport was. Jason said basketball. Cory smiled and said that was his favorite sport too. The boys learned that they lived only two blocks away from each other. They started walking to school together and soon became friends. Jason had felt lonely. His older brother picked on him, and he'd had no one to talk to about it. Jason felt a lot better now that he had a friend to talk to. Jason didn't have to bully others anymore to feel good about himself.

Glossary

accomplishment (uh-KOM-plish-mint) Something that has been done with skill, knowledge, or ability.

bully (BUL-lee) Person who teases, threatens, or hurts smaller people.

comfortable (KUMF-ter-bul) To feel free from pain or hardship.

confront (kun-FRUNT) To meet face-to-face.

frustrated (FRUS-tray-tid) To feel defeated, useless, or worthless.

insult (in-SULT) To say something mean or hurtful to someone on purpose, just to make the person feel bad.

intimidate (in-TIM-ih-dayt) To make someone afraid.

self-esteem (SELF-es-TEEM) Feeling good about yourself.

threat (THRET) Statement of what will be done to hurt someone.

threaten (THREH-tin) When someone uses words to scare you.

Index